How to Write a Great Story

A Guide to Writing Fiction

By Othello Bach

Teacher's Guide

ISBN 10: 1535449950

ISBN 13: 978-1535449953

 Choice Books

Choicebooks4122@gmail.com

Dedication

To all kids who want to write.

Table of Contents

Chapter   Title

Introduction

Many people want to write but are afraid to try. They're fearful because their spelling is weak, their vocabulary is lacking, or perhaps they think they aren't smart enough or don't have the talent. Unfortunately, because they never try, they'll never know.

If you have doubts about your ability to imagine wonderful stories and express your ideas in writing, then perhaps you'll reconsider when you read my story.

I was a non-reader until near the end of the eighth grade. I can only speculate how I managed that, but it was probably because I had been through some pretty rough years before I was six, and by the age of seven was living in an orphanage.

Humiliated by being unable to read, I spent most of my grade school years trying to calculate when I would be called on to read, then conveniently going to the bathroom, moving to an empty desk, creating a disturbance and distracting the teacher, or whatever it took to avoid being exposed and embarrassed. I cheated shamelessly on spelling tests and did hours of extra work for other kids in the orphanage, in exchange for their reading homework assignments to me so that I could at least participate in class discussions. Plus, I developed excellent listening skills.

I had memorized how to spell my first and last names, but in the second grade I had a teacher who wanted us to also put our middle names on our papers. My middle name, Fern, should have been easy to spell but the letters of the alphabet made no sense to me. I knew the four letters in my middle name; I just didn't know their order. So, on the first paper I turned in, using the four letters that I knew spelled *Fern*, I took a stab at it and wrote "N r e f," and hoped I had guess correctly.

When the paper was returned, the teacher had written, in blue pencil, the letters "SP" above it. I didn't know what "SP" meant either, but I figured I'd guessed wrong. So I tried again. On the next paper I wrote *E r f n.* Again, the teacher wrote "SP." The third time, I tried the combination: *F n e r.* When she again wrote *"*SP," it occurred to me that maybe she was trying to tell me how to spell my name! Relieved, I confidently wrote Othello SP James on my next paper and proudly turned it in.

When the teacher handed it back the next day, I sat, dumbfounded, staring at what she had done. She had circled the "SP" and drawn three huge question marks above it. Obviously, she did know how to spell it either, so I quit worrying about it.

Then, in fifth grade, a new girl entered the class. She was introduced to us as "Fern." I could hardly wait for recess. Seizing the opportunity, I rushed up to her with pencil and paper and said, "May I have your autograph?" She nodded, smiled graciously, (as if this happened to her every day), and signed her name. Finally, the problem was solved.

I now had three words I could spell but they fulfilled few homework assignments. So I kept cheating. I traded every possible talent and job in order to get homework completed.

"I'll wash your socks and polish your shoes if you'll do my homework."

"I'll do your laundry and clean your room if you'll write my book report."

Sometimes I had to trade three hours of work for a fifteen-minute assignment, but then, life's tough when you can't read.

Somehow I made it into the eighth grade, still unable to read. Spelling tests were, in my estimation, the cruelest form of torture, requiring more creativity than a reproduction of the Mona Lisa. Every week, I was rechallenged - and defeated - in the same arena. The plan was always the same: to cheat. I was, however, smart enough to realize that my methods of cheating had to vary regularly or I would be exposed.

Then, one day near the end of eighth grade, while using the least imaginative method of cheating, (laying one sheet over another), a miracle of staggering proportions occurred.

The teacher called the first word. I pressed the top sheet hard against the desk, to see the words below more clearly. I located what I hoped was the correct word. The second word was called and I repeated the process. When the third word was called, I did the same.

Then the miracle happened! All three words had begun with the letters "ch," and I heard the similarity in the sounds! I realized what was going on! The first two letters of each word were the same and they sounded the same! Cha... Cha... Cha! The secret had been revealed. The code broken! Letters had sounds assigned to them! I was a reader! I had discovered the world's best-kept secret! Every letter of the alphabet had a secret sound! What a great idea! And who told everyone but me? Was I stupid? Had everyone else figured it out before they could walk, while I did nothing but suck my thumb and stumble around in a soggy diaper?

With a headiness I'd never experienced, I waited breathlessly for class to end so I could check out a book from the library and prove to myself that I could read!

When the bell sounded, I rushed into the room which had previously served no purpose in my life except to humiliate and torment me.

"I wanna check out a book," I said excitedly to the

librarian.

"Which book?" she asked.

Stumped, not knowing a single title, I gaped stupidly at her. I knew that I probably shouldn't check out a "thick" book, so I said, "Oh, ah, about a second-grade book, I think."

Without further questions, the merciful librarian disappeared between the few rows of shelves that comprised our small library and soon returned with a book entitled, "The Mystery of the Little Green Turtle."

Embarrassed to be seen with a "baby" book, I hid it quickly inside my notebook.

Back at the Home, I tried to hide my excitement as I quickly changed clothes and hurried to the kitchen, where I worked. *The book* was all that I could think about. I had it hidden under my pillow and I knew that I could read it! I could figure it out! So, while everyone was busy during dinner, I slipped out to the warehouse and took the flashlight that hung inside the door. I hid it until I'd finished cleaning the kitchen, then sneaked it to my dorm.

Later that night, after the lights were out, I eased the book and flashlight from under my pillow, pulled the covers over my head and began to sound out my first words. I didn't know the sounds for all the letters, but I had a running start on it. Ch was "Cha" and there were thirteen letters in my name. Half of the alphabet! I knew how my name sounded and could figure out which letter made what sound. And almost every word in my book had one or more of those letters.

Oh, the joy! The freedom! I grunted silently, painstakingly uttering idiotic sounds within my head, until words that I had heard... and which made sense within the context of the sentence... began to form complete thoughts and pass information to me. Ink markings on a page began to talk to me! To create pictures inside my head! To tell me things I had never thought before. Things about a little green turtle. Who could have imagined that I would have cared? And yet I did. I loved that little turtle - and he was missing! Where did he go? Did someone steal him? Was he lost forever? Oh, how I wanted him found!

When I finished the book, I lay enthralled. I had reached a high beyond anything I had ever experienced. So *that* was why people read - to find the turtle!

I could hardly wait until I could return that book and check out another. Having now read "The Mystery of the Little Green Turtle," I thought I was prepared to read anything. So the next day, I hurried back into the library and announced, "Now, I want a high school mystery."

The librarian, without bothering to ask me which one, turned to her beloved shelves and brought me Daphne DuMaurier's *Rebecca*. This time, I proudly carried my *thick* book out of the library.

Later that night, huddled under my covers, I reverently turned to the first page. My initial response was horror, but not the kind Ms. DuMaurier had in mind, I'm sure. All of my new-found pride vanished and I stared in shock and dismay at the multi-syllable vocabulary.

But I wanted the thrill back. I wanted the sense of pride and accomplishment I had felt last night, because for those few hours when I thought I could read, I felt like a different - and better! -- person. So sound for sound, syllable for syllable and eventually word for word, I worked at it. When words finally became sentences, and thoughts were being communicated to me, I was overwhelmed with another realization. Words not only passed information -- they created feelings. I was amazed that as I lay there reading, I had grown afraid - afraid because the thoughts being communicated were frightening!

...there was this poor scared lady in this big spooky house and her new husband seemed kind of cold, like he didn't love her much, and there was this scary, awful housekeeper who kept creeping all over the place and she reminded me of the matrons and...

The words, and the ideas they expressed, had created my fear, and the realization astounded me. This was priceless information - maybe even the most important information in the world! - because with it, I could literally change my feelings any time I wanted, and maybe change the direction of my life. Knowing I had discovered something of great value, I considered it carefully, determined to remember and use it.

I struggled with *Rebecca* for months. It took me the remainder of the year to finish it, and I knew that I hadn't really *read* it. Some of the words and phrases just wouldn't make sense, and I wanted to know them. So I kept the book. I read it again the next year. The second time it kept fewer secrets from me. Then, I re-read it the next year. After the third reading, I decided that I now knew the story... had gleaned from the pages the information I needed. I had actually *read* a whole, thick book!

So I didn't bother to read another. By the time I graduated from high school, I was so caught up in my own melodrama that I didn't need any help from hard-to-read books to make life interesting.

I was 22, divorced and with a young son before I decided to read another book. Having been steered toward a so-called "classic," I read the first ten or twelve pages, put it down and decided I could write a better book than that. Taking an old typewriter from the closet, I began to write about my experiences in the orphanage. I wrote what I thought was a short story and sent it off immediately. The editor, who rejected it, also took the time to scribble some advice:

Dear Othello,

Who are you trying to kid? Things like this haven't happened since Dickens wrote about them.

By the way, I suggest you choose a less pretentious pseudonym."

Actually, I wasn't insulted until I looked up a couple of words in the dictionary, then all I could do was shrug. I could change my name but what was I going to do with a past that wasn't believable?

Finally, I decided that if editors weren't interested in what was happening to orphans, I would write whatever they wanted to read. When I became famous, they would be interested in what I had to say about the orphans. With that decided, I set out to become a real writer, to write books like *Rebecca*.

That afternoon, with my son in a stroller at my side, I bought half a dozen books, all with a similar picture on the cover, and which reminded me of *Rebecca*. I had no idea there was a category of fiction called "Gothic," nor that what I had determined to do was write fiction. I just knew that I had to find a way to become rich and famous so I could sell my story about the orphanage.

At home, I read and re-read the books, taking careful notes. There had to be a method, a formula. I was sure of it because every book had 168 pages and all the covers had a frightened woman fleeing from a spooky house.

I jotted down all the similarities between the stories, the number of characters, what kind of work they did, what kind of problems they had, how many complications developed before the problem was solved, how it ended, and so on. When I had finished, I decided to incorporate every similarity into my story. I felt guilty for "cheating" but I was good at that so I did it anyway. (Without knowing it, I figured out how to write formula fiction before I knew such a category existed.)

So all-consuming and blissful was my ignorance that three months later I mailed out my first novel manuscript. With no "dos and don'ts" to slow me down, I never once questioned or doubted that my book was terrific and would sell. I knew it would scare others as much as Daphne DuMaurier had frightened me.

Before starting my second novel, I wrote an article that sold for $35. I hooted and yelp and jumped around all day, celebrating my growing fame. A year later, as I was finishing my second novel, my first novel sold to Avon Books. My second and third novels sold to Zebra Books, and with each sale I yelped and danced and with anyone in sight. On one occasion, it was a man from a pool cleaning service. He had just finished with our pool, when I received the "acceptance" call. Shrieking like a hysterical fool, I ran outside, grabbed the pool man's hands and began to dance. Startled, he allowed me to lead and laughed with me, congratulating me, and eventually left without giving me the bill. He did, however, remember it a few hours later.

Since then I have sold several more books and my response is always the same. Celebrating the sale of a piece of fiction is the purest form of happiness for me because every step of the process is pure. Pure imagination produces it, there is pure joy in creating it, and it is written purely for the sake of entertaining. There is also pure relief when someone buys it.

Writing fictions gives every writer a sense of power and control. To create characters that speak, breathe, love and hate, and then to move them through an exciting plot, creates a deep and unparalleled sense of satisfaction and pride. For this reason, I encourage everyone who enjoys telling stories and dreaming up interesting situations to try writing fiction. Unless you try, you'll never know if it might bring a new and wonderful joy into your life, and into the lives of others, as well.

If I can do it...well, you know the rest.

How to Write a Great Story

A great story is one that keeps your imagination racing and your eyes glued to the page. It keeps you turning pages to see what happens next, and when you realize you're almost to the end, you wish it would go on forever.

A great story has interesting and believable characters, a strong, exciting plot, natural-sounding dialogue and plenty of action to keep the story moving. But no one is born a great writer. Just as it takes years of practice to become an outstanding athlete, dancer, or concert pianist, it takes years of practice to become a great writer. However, if you enjoy using your imagination, the years of practice will go by quickly, and someday, everyone will be reading your stories!

Writing Helps in Many Ways

Learning to write stories in grade school helps you learn how to use your imagination in a way that will benefit you in every other school subject. Plotting a story from beginning to end forces your mind to stay focused on problems until they

13

are solved. Learning to create characters and situations so real that others can see them also builds self-confidence. If you know how to communicate your ideas clearly, you have a powerful skill that will assist you in many ways for the rest of your life.

However, before story writing can be discussed, you will need to learn several terms and phrases. These are words that will help you understand the information presented in this book and make your story writing easier.

Please read through the list of words and phrases below so that when you come to these words later, you'll understand what you are reading.

1) **Character** and **characterization**. A *character* is not a real person, but is someone who is playing a part in a story or play. *Characterization* means "everything about that character," from size and shape to emotion and actions.
2) **Plot** - all of the actions and events of the main story.
3) **Dialogue** - the words the characters speak. Dialogue is always enclosed in quotation marks.
4) **Taglines** - the words that identify who is speaking. The "he said" and "she said" that follows a line of dialogue.
5) **Point of View** - the way things are seen through a character's eyes.
6) **Outline** - A brief statement of the characters and plot. Writers make outlines so that the story will move steadily ahead at all times.
7) **Transition** - a way of moving smoothly from one point in the story to another.
8) **Editing** - rereading and rewriting your story to make it better.
9) **Manuscript** - what your story is called once you've put it on paper.
10) **Fiction** - stories about imaginary situations.

14

All of the words listed above are used in this book. If you need to refresh your memory later you can return to this page and quickly read the meaning again.

Chapter One

It All Begins With a Sentence

Learning to write exciting stories begins with learning to write exciting sentences. The kinds of sentences that you write when answering questions on a school exam do not always have to be exciting. You are writing them to pass information, to let the teacher know you have studied your lessons.

When you set out to write *exciting* sentences, you are writing to paint a word picture for someone else to enjoy. You use words that you might never use when answering questions on a test. You express your thoughts in detail, being as clear and original as you can be.

A great fiction story is a series of pictures captured in words. It allows the reader to meet new characters and visit new places - all people and places you have imagined for them.

Perhaps the best part of fiction writing is that you, the writer, are in complete control of what happens in the world you create. You create the people, their families and homes, and every experience they have. You are the ruler of a tiny universe, where through your words others can visit and experience new and exciting situations.

You may write about a beggar or a rich man, and for the time that you are writing the story, you become that person. You think his thoughts and imagine all of his movements and words. The people in your tiny fiction universe must do what you want them to do, because you are the ruler... the writer who created them.

However, before you can write an exciting story, you must first learn how to write an exciting sentence... then an exciting paragraph. Eventually, however, your mind will be racing with new ways to express your thoughts so that you can show others the wonderful worlds you see.

A Great Sentence

A great sentence is one that forms a perfect picture in the mind of the reader. It does not have to be long and requires no special vocabulary. It merely communicates an idea so perfectly that the reader can see and feel it.

Most young writers have only one way to express their ideas. They use one or two verbs, and these tell the reader nothing. These two over-used verbs are *was* and *were*. While these words are fine if used *occasionally,* if used too often, they will destroy an otherwise good story.

Example

The sun was setting.

While there is nothing wrong with that sentence, there is also nothing new or exciting about it. It tells the reader that it is early evening, but that's all.

With just a little thought and effort, at least part of the sunset could be described by the writer and seen by the reader. If the sunset is worth mentioning, then surely its beauty is worth sharing.

Which of these sentences are more exciting?

The sun was setting.

or...

Long, golden fingers of light stretched across the evening sky and lingered there, as if pointing to tomorrow.

Bill was fat. He was sitting in his chair, watching TV.

or...

When Bill sat in his recliner, the pillow of fat resting on his stomach almost blocked his view of the television.

Sue was walking across the field when she fell down.

or...

Lost in her daydreams, Sue closed her eyes to enjoy the sunshine on her face. She walked with her face up-turned for several steps before she stumbled. Her legs gave way like a marionette whose strings had been cut.

See it, Feel it, Write it.

Before you begin to write a sentence, imagine the scene you want to paint with your words. Imagine you are the character you are writing about, and feel what that character feels. Smell what that character smells and hear with that character's ears. For an instant, before you begin to write, see and feel what you want the reader to see and feel.

Use Exciting Verbs

Bright pictures are painted with bright colors. Exciting stories are told with exciting verbs. Dull verbs such as *was* and *were* are weak and lifeless. Verb phrases such as *had been* and *have been* are even duller. The lack of life in these phrases is enough to kill almost any sentence.

It was almost dark. They had been walking for hours when they reached the farm.

Why not paint a picture the reader can really see?

Darkness slowly overtook the valley as they trudged wearily up the road to the farm.

18

Other dull verbs are:

> walk, walked, walking
>
> talk, talked, talking
>
> sit, sat, sitting
>
> stand, stood, standing
>
> run, ran, running

Everyone walks, talks, sits, stands and runs. To write, *s/he walked across the yard,* tells nothing about your character or his mood. There are many ways of walking, all of them more descriptive than *walk.* You might say, *s/he hurried, strode, trudged, sauntered, ambled, crept, sneaked, or jogged* across the yard. If you do not know these words then describe how he walked by using adjectives. *He walked slowly and with heavy steps. S/He walked quickly with light energy.*

However, it is far better to improve your vocabulary than to rely on adverbs. A strong verb is always better than the best adverb.

But the king of all dull, mindless, say-nothing verbs is the word *got.*

Example

He got sick. She got up and got medicine for him. He got out of bed. She got his robe. They got the door open and got outside right away. He got sick again. She got tired of him getting sick.

Got is useless because it only tells you that *something* happened, but the reader doesn't know what. Look at how much more information the reader receives when action verbs replace the word *got*.

He fainted. She sprang up and grabbed his medicine. Awaking slowly, he pushed himself up. She draped his robe over his shoulders, then opened the door. They stepped outside. Immediately, he became ill again. She sighed, growing weary of his constant sickness.

Verbs are action words. Choose verbs that show the action you have in mind for your character.

Exercise - Part 1

Beside each word (walk, talk, sit, stand, run) write at least three others verbs that have a close or similar meaning but create an action picture in your mind.

Ask students to complete part two of the exercise. Allow students to share their rewritten sentences.

Part 2 - Rewrite the sentences below, using strong action verbs to replace the weak verbs in the sentences.

Julie sat down. Sam stood in the doorway. Later, they got ice cream and left.

The sun got hot. It was right overhead. Mike was tired and wanted to sit in the shade of the big oak tree.

Tammy walked over to see Tom. They talked for a long time. George was walking over to talk with Tammy when a black cat ran right in front of him.

Chapter Two

Sentence Length

Words do more than paint pictures; they also create emotions within the reader. Carefully chosen words and well-thought-out sentences can make the reader feel frightened, depressed, happy, or sad.

Even the length of a sentence helps to create a mood within the reader. Long sentences with several "ing" words slow down the pace of the story. Short sentences with strong, powerful verbs create a sense of action. Knowing this, you can actually slow the readers' minds and help them relax and enjoy the sunset that you painted with words. You can also speed up their minds and make them race when you want them to feel excited.

Example

Easing his head slowly onto the pillow, Jim marveled at how wonderful the bed felt beneath his tired, aching body. The pillow, caressing his head like a loving mother, comforted him as he allowed the exhausting tension to flow out of his arms, legs and back.

Or...

Startled, Jim sprang up. The phone rang again. He fumbled for the receiver. It slipped from his hand and clattered to the floor. He grabbed it. "Yes? Yes?" He shook his head and tried to wake up.

If you are careful to select words that paint the exact picture you have in mind, and pay attention to the length of your sentences, you can help the reader see the scene more clearly.

Sentence Structure

Sentence *structure* is the way you arrange the words in a sentence. To make a paragraph interesting, you need to arrange the words in the sentences so that each one is a little different.

Example *of poor* sentence structure

The bed was against one wall. The chair was against the other wall. The dresser was against the third wall. The closet took up all of the fourth wall.

In the paragraph above, every sentence is structured the same. As you can see, this makes for pretty boring reading. Even if you continued to use the verb "was" in almost every sentence, the structure still needs to be varied. You do this by changing the arrangement of the words. Instead of always mentioning the subject (noun) first, use an occasional inverted sentence. An inverted sentence has all or part of the predicate (verb) before the subject (noun).

Example

The bed was against one wall. The other wall had only a chair next to it. Standing against the third wall was a bed. Nothing was on the fourth wall except a closet.

You could, of course, take the time to paint a picture so that the reader can really see the room. You do this by describing the items in the room and using strong verbs that help the reader see what you want them to see.

Example

The shabby little room had only a few pieces of furniture. Without a window, the furnishings almost faded into the shadows. A small, unmade bed, its mattress sagging, squatted against the far wall. A tired, old chair and long dresser

22

crouched humbly against the other walls, as if wanting to hide from the shame of their many scars and scratches. The open bottom drawers of the dresser suggested someone had emptied them in a hurry. The small, dark closet held nothing but a single warped hanger.

✔ *Writing Exercise*

When students have completed part one of the exercise, ask them to share the rewritten sentences aloud.

Exercises

Part 1 - Rewrite the sentences below. Describe this room so that readers will feel as if they have seen it with their own eyes.

There was a table in the room. It had a book on it. There was a sofa, too. The end table had a vase of flowers on it. The flowers were dead.

Part 2 - Describe your own room so that readers will feel as if they've seen it. Write at least five sentences.

Part 3 - Describe a grandmother's or grandfather's room. Write at least five sentences.

Assignment: Have students bring a favorite fiction book to the next class.

Chapter Three

Learning From Others

One of the quickest ways to become a great writer is to study the writings of great writers. Working from a book that you like, open it to one of your favorite paragraphs. Keep the book open so that you can look at that paragraph as you write. Then, using the paragraph as a guide, pattern your own paragraph after it. Rewrite each sentence carefully, changing words to make them fit your scene.

Example

(A paragraph from a book.)

The sun warmed Helen as she skipped down the road to her grandmother's house. Little puffs of dust rose from the ground with every step she took. Her mind raced excitedly as she thought of going into town with her grandmother. Days of shopping with her were always fun.

This is how you might rewrite it.

The rain poured down on John as he ran along the sidewalk to his aunt's apartment. Puddles splashed beneath his feet with every step. He dreaded days spent with his aunt. They were never any fun.

By using the paragraph as a pattern for what you might do, your writing becomes better. You are forced to describe the scene so that others can see it. However, because you have changed the characters and everything in the scene, the new scene is your own.

✔ *Writing Exercise*

Part 1 - Using the following paragraph as a guide, rewrite it.

24

use the same sentence structure but change the details.

The old lady leaned heavily on her cane as she slowly made her way to the bus bench. She wore a floppy brimmed hat to shield her from the sun and a pair of sunglasses so big, they covered half of her face. She dropped to the bench as though she had taken her last step and never intended to move again.

Part 2

Copy a paragraph from one of your favorite books, the rewrite it, using the same sentence structure but changing the details.

Chapter Four

What kind of story should you write?

Always write about something that interests *you*. What kind of stories do you like to read? Do you like mysteries or love stories? Adventure stories or horror tales? Perhaps you like science fiction or westerns. Whatever it is, *that's* the kind of story you should write. Trying to write a story you don't like is a waste of time because no one else will like it, either.

How to Create Characters

The characters in your story are much more than just names and bodies. While a character's name and the color of his/her hair and eyes may be important, a great character is much more.

The age, size and shape of your characters are not nearly as important as their emotions. However, there are times when your character's physical appearance plays a part in your story. When it does, take the time to describe your character so that readers will feel they see a photograph. Point out details that will create a "word snapshot."

Most young writers think that telling the color of a character's hair, eyes, and shirt or dress is enough to make the reader see the character. It is not.

Example

He had dark hair and wore a yellow shirt. She had on a pink skirt and blouse to match.

The color and type of clothing is only a small part of your character's description and frequently it is not needed at all. For clothing to matter, it must say something about your character. How does that blue dress fit or that green shirt hang on your character's body? Is the character comfortable or ill-at-ease? If the weather is hot, is your character perspiring or uncomfortable? Are there damp spots on his shirt?

Example

The large dark coat swallowed her, making it obvious that it was a hand-me-down.

Or...

He tugged nervously at his shirtsleeves, self-conscious that they were too short.

You may also use various props from the environment to help describe your character. Let the sun, wind, rain, and other objects in the room, help define him.

Example

As Sally leaned against the open door, a sudden gust of wind rushed in. Her long red hair fanned about her face and danced in the lingering breeze. Her green summer dress swirled about her knees but she didn't seem to notice. "That's nice," she said, lifting her face to air. "I'm glad it's cooling off."

Or...

Tommy squatted in front of the TV, looking up only occasionally as he played with the kitten. His tee shirt and cut-offs were almost as dirty as his feet.

In the first example, the doorway where Sally leaned *and* the wind are used to help describe her character. Leaning shows that she is either tired or relaxed. Her response to the wind tells us she has been too warm. Using the wind to fan her hair about her face is a way to describe her hair without saying

27

something dull, such as: *Sally had long, red hair.*

In the second example, the TV is an environmental prop. It helps to show Tommy as an average kid. What he is doing and what he is wearing also tell us that he's an ordinary kid. Using the TV and kitten help the reader to see more of Tommy than just his clothes. These things also tell us what Tommy enjoys doing.

✔ Writing Exercise

Describe the following characters. Use props (details of the environment) when you can. Write at least four sentences about each character. Since no one knows these characters, you can make up anything you like about them.

A girl or boy caught in a rainstorm.

An old man or woman getting off a bus.

A father or mother leaving for work.

A mother or father just getting up in the morning.

Your Character's Emotions

Readers want to know how characters *feel* about what is happening -- and they don't want the writer to just tell them. They want the writer to *show* them, to let the characters *act out* what they are feeling. This means that the writer must show each character's feelings by describing how he or she walks, talks and acts.

This may sound difficult, but it's not. You already know everything you need to know to do this. Can you tell when someone is sad, even though he or she is not crying? Usually, you can. You can tell by the way that person moves, talks, sits and responds to the things happening around him or her.

Example

The character is Carla, age eight. See if you can tell that she is sad, even though her sadness is never mentioned.

Carla slumped against the fence like a rag doll. Wind whipped long strands of hair across her face, wiping away her tears. She stared at her feet, afraid to look at the kids playing on the other side of the schoolyard.

In three sentences, the reader can clearly see a very sad little girl. They don't know why she's afraid to look up at the other kids, but she is feeling so terrible about something that the reader wants to know what has happened.

Show it. Don't *tell* it.

It is always better to *show* how a character is feeling *by describing how he or she is acting,* than to tell the reader: *Carla was sad. She sat against the fence and cried.*

However, before you can show how a character feels, you must first stop and think about how people act in different moods and situations. To do this, think about how you would feel in different situations. Think about the different parts of your body and how they respond to your emotions.

How do you act and how does your body respond when you're afraid?

What happens to your heart? Does it pump hard and fast?

What happens to your breathing? Does it become more rapid? Do you feel out of breath?

What happens to your hands? Do they become sweaty and sort of cold and clammy?

What about your mouth? Does it go dry?

Do you open your eyes very wide... or blink rapidly?

Do you tremble and shake or become stiff as a board?

When you try to talk, how does your voice sound? Does it grow shaky and weak?

The reason that it is easy to write about emotions is that everyone has them and almost everyone responds the same way.

Example

Miss Clark slammed the book down. Hands on her hips, she glared at the students. "All right!" she snapped, "I've had just about enough of this nonsense!"

Did you know that Miss Clark was angry, even though there is no mention of her anger? Were her actions enough to convince you that she was angry?

You know Miss Clark is angry because everyone who feels angry, does some of those things. She could have done more. She could have snorted hard. She might have screamed and pounded the table. She might even have been trembling. We know all of this because these are the actions of someone who is angry.

When a writer takes the time to *show* how a character is feeling, the character "comes alive" for the reader. The reader can see and feel the character's emotions.

Before writing a scene about an angry person, think about what happens to your body when you are angry:

Do your shoulders sag or do you pull them up like you're

ready to fight?

Does your chest become hollow or suddenly puff out?

How does anger affect your breathing? Do you talk in a soft voice and long sentences, or does your voice become loud and your words come out short and quick?

Do you think clearly or do your thoughts come too quickly and shoot out of your mouth too soon?

Does your face and neck redden? Do you shake?

To help you remember all the ways your body responds to your emotions, think about each part of your body and what happens to it when you experience different feelings. For instance, what happens to your body and your actions when you are sad?

✔ *Writing Exercise*

Part 1- List some of the ways your body responds when you are sad, angry, or frightened.

Part 2 - After you have listed these responses, write three or four sentences showing how these characters feel and act.

Use these responses to write three or four sentences describing how the following characters feel and act.

1) *Sammy, age 9, is sitting in the principal's office. He knows he's in big trouble. (Do **not** say he is scared or sad. **Show it.**)*

2) *Rachel, age 12, has lost her dog. What is she feeling? How does she act? What does she do?*

3) *Mr. or Mrs. Martin is furious because someone has stolen his/her newspaper. How does s/he act? What does s/he do*

and say?

4) *Julie, age 12, is very happy. She has just learned that her parents who were divorced are getting back together. Show how she feels. Describe how she acts.*

5) *Tim, age 14, is angry because his sister has read a note from his girlfriend.*

Chapter Five

Characterization Through Environment

Describing your characters' environment tells the reader a lot about them. The way they decorate their rooms and homes, and even how they keep the house - whether it's clean or messy - tells the reader what kind of person a character is.

Example

Mary stretched across her unmade bed as she talked on the telephone. Rumpled sheets and blankets twisted around her legs when she moved. Several cola cans and dirty paper plates littered the floor. A half-eaten piece of pizza, dried and curling around the edges, stained the carpet beneath the bed. Clean and dirty clothing was strewn about the room, piled on top of books, papers, and candy wrappers.

It's easy to see that Mary is a slob. But it's a lot more fun for the reader if the writer *shows* that Mary is a slob instead of just telling about it.

Look at the difference. The paragraph below is an *example of **telling**, instead of **showing***.

Mary is a slob. She never makes her bed. She leaves dirty paper plates and empty cola cans all over her room. She also never picks up her clothes and leaves candy wrappers everywhere.

Readers do not want to be *told* anything. They want the writer to show them how it is and what is happening. Only then, can the reader see the scene in his or her mind, and know exactly what is going on.

✔ Writing Exercise

Describe Mark's room, using the information below.

Mark is a neatness freak. Everything must be perfect in his room. Follow the example given in the description of the dirty room. Begin with Mark on the bed. Describe the bed. Show what is on the floor. Describe his clothing, shoes, and show how everything in the room is put away where it belongs.

A Sympathetic Character

Sympathetic characters are good people who have problems, so it's easy to have sympathy for these characters. Because they are good, we want them to solve their problems. Most stories are about sympathetic characters. When a sympathetic character is also the main character, he or she is called a *protagonist.*

The person who is causing all the problems in a story is called an *antagonist.* An antagonist is an opponent, trying to stop or hinder the success of the main character, or the protagonist.

How to Show Character Strengths and Weaknesses

One way to show the reader what kind of person your character is, is to show your character in a scene with another character who is not as strong or big - such as a pet or young friend. A kind person - or character - will treat others with kindness, even when no one is around. Unkind, or cruel people, may be kind when others are around, but they will be unkind when no one is watching.

Example - of *showing* your character as kind.

Jimmy crouched down to peek under the bushes. A kitten's wide, frightened eyes stared back at him. "Here, kitty. Come here," he whispered, gently sliding his fingers beneath the bush. "Come here. I'll feed you."

Of course, you could have told the reader, "Jimmy was a kind boy," but that wouldn't have been nearly as interesting.

Example - of *showing* your character is unkind.

George knelt beside the bush as silently as he could. Through the branches he could see the kitten. It stared at him with wide, frightened eyes. "Get!" he yelled suddenly shaking the bush as hard as he could. "Get away from my house!"

You could have written, "George was unkind, even to kittens." Which do you think is more interesting to read?

✔ *Writing Exercise*

Write a scene showing how kind and unkind characters handle the same situation. Your characters may be men, women or children.

1) Your character sees a young child who needs help.

2) A bird flies into your character's room.

3) Your character discovers a turtle on its back.

Making Your Characters Believable

Believable characters respond to life in the same way that real people respond. Because everyone's mood changes from time to time, your character will have different moods throughout your story. As the story plot progresses, your character's emotions will change. When things are going well, s/he will feel good and see the whole world through the eyes of someone who is feeling good. His or her point of view will be happy and positive.

When things are not going well for your character, his or

her point of view will not be positive. Just as you see things differently when things are not going well, so will your characters. Also, like you, when your character's mood changes, actions and responses will also change.

Example

Character: Sam, age 14

Situation: Sam is just arriving home from school. He's happy because his report card is filled with A's and B's. He's never received such good grades.

The front door was stuck again. Sam leaned against it and nudged it open. Inside, he looked around at the empty living room. The old couch invited him to sit awhile. The pictures on the mantle of his grandparents smiled down at him as if they were proud of the report card in his pocket. Moving to the window, Sam opened the blinds and let the sun stream in, brightening the room. This is a good house, he thought. I can't wait for Mom and Dad to come home.

Example

Character: Sam, age 14

Situation: Sam is just arriving home from school. He's sad and angry about his report card. It's filled with all D's and F's.

The front door was stuck again. Furious, Sam slammed his body against it. It crashed open. Inside, he stared at the empty living room. The old couch looked dirty and uncomfortable. The pictures on the mantle of his grandparents seemed to mock him. He could practically hear them saying, "You're such a stupid boy, Sam." Moving to the window, Sam closed the blinds even tighter. He wanted to disappear into the darkness of this ugly, old house, and never have to face his parents again.

As you can see, the two scenes are exactly alike, except for the character's mood. When Sam's mood changes, everything seems different. Nothing in the room actually changes. It is only Sam's perspective that makes the room seem different.

✔ *Writing Exercise*

Write about the situations presented below. First, describe the room from the character's happy perspective, then describe it from an unhappy perspective.

1)   It's your character's birthday. S/he has just had a great party. Describe your character's room from his or her happy point of view.
2)   It's your character's birthday. No one came to the party. Describe your character's room from his/her unhappy point of view.
3)   Your character has just won a trip to Disneyland. S/he is sitting in the kitchen. Describe it from this happy point of view.
4)   Your character was promised a trip to Disneyland. The promise has been broken. S\he or she is sitting in the kitchen. Describe it from that unhappy point of view.

Creating Memorable Characters

The best characters are those the reader remembers forever. One of the ways to create memorable characters is to make them *different*. Fortunately, there are two ways to do that. The first is to make them physically different, such as *Superman* or *The Ugly Duckling*. The second way is to make them mentally or emotionally different. Characters who are mentally or emotionally different do not think and act like everyone else. Consequently, we love them or hate them more than other characters.

Do you remember how strongly you felt about *The Little Engine That Could?* This was probably one of the first stories you ever heard or read. Children have loved it since the day it was written because the little engine in *The Little Engine That Could* is mentally and emotionally *different*. He refuses to quit, and readers love a character that is determined and *different*.

Think about your favorite TV programs for a minute and you'll see that the characters you like best are always different. Sometimes the difference is physical and other times it's mental or emotional.

Making the Unbelievable Believable

If you want to create a super hero, such as Superman, you must explain how your character came to have supernatural powers. With Superman, it is said that he comes from another planet. Sometimes super heroes - and super monsters - are made by insane scientists. *How* your character becomes super isn't as important as telling the reader - in the *first of the story* - which something happened to give the character supernatural power. Even if your reason is not too believable, the readers will accept it if you present it "up front." If you do not explain it quickly, the readers will think *you* are crazy for expecting them to believe that such a super person exists.

Example

Jan stared at the door, afraid to knock. She had to warn Mrs. Scott to stay away from Hampton Street tomorrow. She couldn't go near it... not if she wanted to stay alive. But how would she tell her without sounding like a crazy person? Even if she told her the truth--which every time she put on the sunglasses she found in the alley she could see the future--she wouldn't believe her. Who would? Jan could hardly believe it herself.

˅ *Writing Exercise*

Write an opening paragraph about a character that is able to make dead plants come alive and grow again. Show the character using this super power and explain how s/he came to have it.

Different Thoughts and Emotions

When creating a character who thinks differently than others, it is not so necessary to explain. The character's words and actions often convince the reader that he or she is not only different, but good or bad.

Heidi, in the book *Heidi*, is different because even when she's in situations where others would cry and complain, she accepts them and makes the best of them. Consequently, readers like her. They can see that she's different from them, but they know it would be possible to see things as she does, if they wanted to. So while Heidi is different, she is not unbelievable.

In *The Christmas Carol* by Charles Dickens, the character Scrooge is definitely different. He is meaner and more heartless than most people. This doesn't have to be explained either because everyone knows what it is to feel mean and heartless to others. Everyone has done it at one time or another.

Going from Bad to Good

(Motivation for Change)

When your story is about a bad or mean character that has a change of heart and becomes a good, generous character, you must explain the change of heart - a*nd the explanation must be believable.* In *The Christmas Carol*, Scrooge has a series of dreams or "visions" in which he sees terrible things that make him afraid. He becomes convinced that he had better change or he's headed for big trouble.

In real life, people do not change their minds or their ways easily. They must be convinced that they are wrong and that it would benefit them to change. The same is true for your characters. If your main character is a "bad guy" and you want him to have a change of heart and become a "good guy," you must convince him (and the reader) that he has "learned his lesson" and changed his mind.

✔ *Writing Exercise*

Part 1 - *Your character is able to turn him/herself into many different things, such as a tree, a thunderstorm, or an ant. First, explain how s/he is able to do this and show the character using this power for good or bad.*

Part 2 - *Your character is terrified of cats. Show your character in a scene with a cat, then tell the reader why s/he is terrified. You may do this by having the character remember a terrible incident with a cat or by having someone else explain your character's strange behavior.*

Part 3 - *Your character is a very poor student and is rude to the teacher and other students. What things happen to make your character have a change of heart and want to be a better student and better person?*

Chapter Six

Writing Great Dialogue

The words that your characters speak are called *dialogue*. Dialogue is always enclosed in quotation marks ("Help!"). When the speaker changes, you must indent and start a new paragraph so you will not confuse the reader.

Dialogue is the one area of writing where characters are quite different from life. In real life, people can sit for hours, talking about nothing important. They may bore themselves and each other, and in real life, that's okay. People who love each other are interested in all the details of their friends' and families' lives. They babble on endlessly. However, when you are writing a story, every word of dialogue must be important to your story. If your characters blabber on and on, they will bore your reader, who will stop reading your story.

The Purpose of Dialogue

There are only two reasons for dialogue: 1) to make the character fuller and more real, and 2) to give the reader information about the plot. Any line of dialogue that doesn't do one of these two things should be eliminated. Never waste time involving your characters in unnecessary conversations.

To write great dialogue you must pay attention to the way people talk. Everyone speaks a little differently. Even within families, each person has a way of speaking that is somewhat different from other family members.

Some people talk in long, drawn-out sentences and use a lot of words to say the simplest things. Others speak in short, quick sentences and use only a few words. There are people who never use more than two syllable words and others who want to impress everyone with their huge vocabulary.

As the writer of the story, you must decide how you want your characters to talk. You must also know how you want the characters' voices to sound when they speak, and whether their voices should be soft or loud, high or low.

The best way to "test" your dialogue to see if it sounds natural is to read it out loud. If, when you read it, it sounds unnatural, then delete it and write another line.

Example of unnatural dialogue.

"Will you come and help me, please? I am drowning."

The line of dialogue is unnatural because a person who is drowning can hardly breathe, much less talk. A drowning person would also be panicked. The only *natural* dialogue in this situation would be: "Help! I'm drowning!"

Which line of dialogue sounds most natural to you?

"Oh, dear. I think you might need to stop the car. My stomach doesn't seem to like my lunch."

Or...

"Stop the car! I'm gonna throw up!"

When some characters speak, they will always use correct English. If you have a teacher in your story, the teacher will always talk like a teacher, using correct grammar. But if you are writing about children, or people who are not educated and do not always speak correctly, you will give them lines of dialogue which are natural and realistic to them.

Example of a teacher asking to borrow a pencil.

"John, may I borrow your pencil, please?"

Example of another student asking to borrow a pencil.

42

"Hey, John! Gotta pencil?"

It takes only a little thought to know how to write natural sounding dialogue.

✔ *Writing Exercise*

Write lines of dialogue to fit these situations:

A mother or father is running after her two-year-old who is about to run into the street.

A girl/boy is late for school and can't find his/her homework.

A boy/girl is angry because a friend has broken his/her radio.

A police officer is telling a troublemaker to leave of the park.

Dialogue and Taglines

"Taglines" are the lines that identify which character is speaking.

Example

*"Get me a piece of rope," **Jim said.***

*"I can't find any rope," **said Mary.***

*"But I need a piece of rope!" **Jim insisted.***

*"Then go buy some!" **Mary replied.***

Simple taglines such as "he said" and "she replied" do not tell the reader much about the character, and they can become very tiresome if used too frequently. Sometimes, however, they are necessary. Great writers have several ways of identifying the speaker. One of the best ways to "tag" the speaker is to give the speaker a line of action following the line of dialogue.

Dialogue and Physical Action.

As your characters talk, they will also move. Hardly anyone speaks without some sort of movement in other parts of the body. We use our hands. We swing our feet. We walk around, pick up things, keep working or watching TV. People move as they talk, so you will want to remember to keep your characters moving. It will make their dialogue seem more real and natural, and keep your reader interested in what is being said.

In the following example, you'll see how the action lines make John and Mary's conversation seem more alive.

Example

"Get me a piece of rope." Jim sat on the suitcase to hold it shut.

Mary ran to the garage, but returned empty-handed. "I can't find any."

Jim glanced around the room, scowling. "But I need a piece of rope!"

Mary laughed. "Then go buy some."

The scene is more interesting because the characters are moving and acting as they speak.

When the characters have longer lines of dialogue, you can also make the scene more interesting by breaking up the dialogue with your action lines. You can also add more action.

Example

"Get me a piece of rope." Jim sat on the suitcase to keep it closed. "This thing won't stay shut unless I tie it."

Mary hurried to the garage but returned empty-handed. "I can't find any." She handed him a ball of string. "Will this help?"

Jim scowled at her. "No. It's not strong enough. I have to have rope."

Mary shrugged. "Then I guess you'll have to buy some." With a flip of her head, she left the room.

Contractions

Another way to make your character's dialogue sound natural is to use contractions. Since most people use contractions when they speak, most of your characters should, too. In real life, very few people say, "I will do that." Most will say, "I'll do that." They'll say, "Let's go," instead of "Let us go." If you read your dialogue out loud, you will catch this mistake.

Sentence Fragments

To write natural sounding dialogue, you must write it the way most people speak in real life, and most of us do not speak in complete sentences all of the time.

Example

"Want to go to the movies?"

"Which one?"

"It doesn't matter."

"Maybe later. Not right now."

Or..

"Where have you been?"

"Out."

"Out where?"

"Just out."

We all understand these fragmented sentences because we speak this way most of the time. As you write your dialogue scenes, remember to use contractions, and if a sentence fragment sounds more natural than a complete sentence, use it.

Also remember that dialogue is used to 1) strengthen the character, or 2) further the plot.

Keep in mind that your scenes will be more alive if you keep your characters moving.

At this point, you do not have a story plot for your characters to discuss in a dialogue scene. However, you can still write good dialogue scenes between two characters, using one of the plot situations below.

Example

Two girls were planning a surprise party for their friend, Jeff.

Betsy ran down the school hall. "Hey, Sharon! Wait for me."

Sharon stopped and looked back. "Oh, good! You're just the person I wanted to see."

"Have you figured out how to get Jeff to your house without him catching on?" Betsy whispered.

Sharon sighed and shook her head.. "Not yet. Everything I've thought of sounds so silly." She moved toward the door. "That's why I wanted to talk to you. What do you think I should say?"

✔ *Writing Exercise*

Write at least four lines of dialogue about the situations presented below. Use action lines instead of taglines to identify the speakers. Before you begin to write, decide what the characters are doing.

1) Jessica is ten. Her pet bird flew away and she is telling her friend, Mia.

2) Charlie, age twelve, is asking George to help him fix his bike.

When you need no tag lines

Earlier, you read that *most* dialogue scenes are better if action lines are added. There are times, however, when no taglines *or* action lines are needed. When a scene is moving quickly and the characters are involved in a conversation, you want the dialogue to move quickly, too. If you add taglines and actions lines to these scenes, you will slow them down and ruin your scene.

Example

Scene: Alan, age six, dropped a quarter and is looking for it. Tim, age ten, walks by, sees the quarter, and picks it up.

"That's my quarter."

"I don't think so."

"Yes, it is! I just dropped it!"

"I don't believe you. You just saw it when I picked it up!"

"No! That's not true! I dropped it a few seconds ago! I was

looking for it!"

"Ha! Well, it's mine now. Finders Keepers!"

In this conversation, taglines are not needed because it is clear who is speaking at all times. When taglines are unnecessary, or when they would only slow down an otherwise fast-action scene, don't use them.

When characters are very different, and it is not possible they can be confused, taglines are not needed.

Example

"All right, young lady! I told you to stay out of the cookie jar!"

"But I was hungry!"

"It's almost lunch time! Give me that cookie!"

"But I want it!"

✔ *Writing Exercise*

Write dialogue scenes that require no taglines. (Remember... because the characters are very different, they should also use different words and have different sentence patterns. If the characters are the same age, but are on opposite sides of an argument, you should be able to write dialogue so the reader will not be confused about who is speaking.)

Remember to use quotation marks and indent each time you change speakers.

A police officer and a little child

A teacher and a first grader

Two angry people arguing

Chapter Seven

How to Plot A Story

Every fiction story needs a plot. The series of problems that the character faces, and his or her attempts to solve those problems, is what makes a story interesting. Without the problems, and the characters trying to solve them, you have only a situation. Situations can be interesting, but not for long. A great story holds the reader's interest for hours, or even days.

The first thing to remember about plotting is *every story must open with a problem.* Not just any character's problem - but the main character's problem. The only exception to this rule is when the main character is a detective or a very close family member. Otherwise, it is not believable that someone would struggle with another person's problem. The detective will struggle with it for money. Family members might struggle with a problem because of their deep love for the one in trouble. But in most stories, the problem always belongs to the main character, and, in the end, the main character must solve his or her own problem.

The following formula will help you develop your own plots. The formula is simple, but to make the plot exciting and believable, you'll have to give the problem some thought.

1) The story must open with the main character's problem.
2) The main character tries to solve the problem.
3) The problem is not solved but worsens.
4) The main character tries again to solve the problem.
5) This attempt does not work either. The problem worsens.
6) The main character tries once more and this time solves the problem.

Who Solves the Problem?

In great stories, the main character always solves his/her own problem. Unless you are writing a fairy tale where magic is happening throughout the story, you cannot use magic to solve the problem in the end.

Solving your character's problems takes thought. Just as you cannot solve it through magic, you cannot solve it with a coincidence. For instance, if your character is looking for her lost dog throughout the entire story, your reader will feel cheated if your story ends with someone saying, "Oh, by the way, I found a great dog today. Is it yours?"

Your characters must work to solve their problems, just like real people.

If your character is trapped in a cave and the bad guys are coming, you must think of a way for your character to save him/herself. It is not acceptable to have a bear come out of the woods and eat the bad guys. Even in fairy tales, this is not acceptable.

Read the examples below and see how even the simplest fairy tales follow this formula.

Example

The Three Little Pigs

1) *Opening problem:* A wolf wants to eat the three little pigs.

2) *Attempted solution:* Pigs close the door.

3) *Problem worsens:* Wolf blows the straw house down.

4) *Attempted solution:* Pigs build a stronger (stick) house.

5) 5) *Problem worsens:* Wolf blows down the stick

house.

6) *Attempted solution:* Pigs build a brick house.

7) *Solution (Climax):* Wolf comes down chimney and lands in boiling pot.

Example

Jack and the Beanstalk

1) *Opening problem:* Jack's family is poor and hungry.

2) *Attempted solution:* He sells the cow for magic beans.

3) *Problem worsens:* Mom is furious and tosses the beans out the window.

4) *Attempted solution:* A tall beanstalk grows overnight. Jack climbs it.

5) *Problem* worsens: Jack finds a giant with a goose that lays golden eggs.

6) *Attempted solution:* Jack takes goose and runs from giant.

7) *Solution (Climax):* Jack cuts beanstalk and kills giant.

Plots Must GrowMore and More Exciting

A plot must become more exciting as the story progresses. As the main character struggles to solve the problem, the reader should care more about him/her. The most exciting part is always the ending, which is called a climax.

If you were to make a diagram of a plot, it would look something like the illustration on the next page.

Plot Diagram

X - Solve it!

O - Try again to solve it.

X - Problem worsens.

O - Try to solve it again.

X - The problem worsens.

O - Try to solve it.

X - Open with a problem.

Short story problems can be solved after one or two attempts, but in longer stories and novels, the main character will have to try several times before solving the problem. Otherwise, your story will not be believable.

Also notice that the plot diagram moves from the bottom to the top of the page. That's because the tension and excitement of a story should continue to build until the very last moment.

How To Find a Great Story Problem

Problems for story plots are everywhere and in every situation you can imagine. Everyone has problems from time to time, so a good story problem is one that you and the reader have experienced.

Children have problems at home with parents, brothers and

53

sisters, neighbors, and even pets. Problems come up at school with teachers, other students, and with the work the students are expected to do.

Problems can also arise within the world, such as being caught in a terrible storm, or running into trouble when stopping to rescue a stranded animal. A problem can arise in any situation. But not all solutions make good story endings. Most readers like a story with a happy ending.

Sometimes good people make mistakes. Many stories are about good characters that make bad decisions - or mistakes. When this happens, the character must come to understand that he has made a mistake, and know how to prevent it from happening again. In other words, the character grows and matures. This allows the reader to grow and mature, too.

When looking for a story problem, just think of the kinds of problems you and your friends have.

The list, below, may give you an idea.

1) Parents divorcing.
2) Parents not having enough money.
3) Kids cheating or being tempted to lie, cheat or steal.
4) Friends and relationships at school.
5) A brother or sister is sneaking around doing drugs.

What If It Went This Way...

Learning to plot means learning to think in a clear, logical way. It means creating a believable problem, then solving it with a believable solution. Once you have decided which problem you want to write about, one of the best ways to plot your story is to ask yourself some "what if" questions.

Let's say you have decided to write the story of The Three

Little Pigs. Imagine that it hasn't been written yet, and it's entirely your idea.

You might say to yourself...

The opening problem is that three little pigs are being threatened by a wolf who wants to eat them.

Now, what if... one of the little pigs decided to save himself by helping the wolf catch the other two pigs?

What if... he helped the wolf blow down other two pigs' house?

What if... the little pigs escaped and knew they needed a stronger house?

What if... the bad little pig helped to blow that house down, too?

What if... what if... what if?

As you can see, a story can be plotted any way you want it, from beginning to end, by asking yourself... "What if this happened," or "What if that happened?" or "What if neither of those things happened, but something else did?"

Writing Exercise

Using the story of The Three Little Pigs, write a new story by asking yourself "What if" until the plot is finished. You may use the "what if" plot started above, or write a new one.

Chapter Eight

Plotting on the Action Scenes

Great stories have great characters that solve problems through great action. When story problems are all mental -- that is, all inside the main character's head -- the story is not exciting. The excitement in your story will come from the action that the main character takes as he or she tries to solve the problems.

An action scene is just what you think it might be: a scene with a lot of physical action. Characters are doing things... moving, talking, running, hiding, trying to escape then trying to return. Good characters are running from bad characters and bad characters are running from good characters.

When they are not physically doing something to solve their problems, they are thinking about what they will do next. This is the "attempted solution" part of the formula.

Examples

George gripped the bat. His heart pounded. Sweat trickled down his neck. He had to hit a home run. He had to! If he didn't do it now, they would lose. If he did do it now, with the bases loaded, they win!

Sam wound up to pitch. George gulped. His knees shook. Then Sam turned loose of the ball and it sped toward the plate. George waited an instant. It was a perfect pitch. He swung hard. The contact jolted his arms and stung his hands. The crowd roared!

"Yes!" He shouted. "Yes!" Charging toward first base, he yelped with joy. The ball sailed right out of the ballpark.

Example

Julie knew she would be in trouble if anyone saw her, but she had to do it. She had to know if old Miss Whittaker was really a witch.

Slipping around the side of the house, she could hardly breathe. In the darkness, the bushes seemed to grab at her. They scratched her legs, snagged her skirt.

"What do you want?" Miss Whittaker's scratchy voice shrieked. "What are you doing here?

Frantically, Julie glanced around. The voice seemed to come from everywhere at once.

"Git!" the old woman shouted. "Or I'll eat you for breakfast tomorrow!

Shoving herself away from the house, Julie's legs flew across the yard. She scrambled over the fence and fell to the other side. Crying and shaking, she pushed herself up and stumbled toward home.

The old woman has to be a witch, she thought. No one else would say such a thing!

Writing Exercise

Write at least three paragraphs of an action scene. Use strong verbs and short sentences to make the action seem greater. You may write a scene of your own, or choose one from the list below.

Someone is being chased by a dog.

A girl or boy is trying to save a cat.

A boy sees a stranger taking his bicycle.

Who Will Tell Your Story?

Generally, the best stories are told from the point of view of the character who is involved in the most action. If you tell it from the point of view of someone who knows the main character and wants to report what happened, your story will not be as exciting as it could be. So decide which character will be involved in the most action, and write your story from his or her point of view. Usually, this is the main character.

There are two ways to tell a story. You may tell it as though it happened to you. This is called a "first person" point of view. This means you will use the words "I" and "me."

Example

I hurried toward the bus, hoping it wouldn't leave without me.

The other way to tell a story is called a "third person" or "omniscient narrator" point of view. That means that you will tell the story from someone else's point of view. You will use the words "he" or "she" or "him" or "her." With the third person point of view you may also tell the story through more than once character's eyes.

Example

Tom hurried toward the bus, hoping it wouldn't leave without him. Jim watched from inside the bus and hoped he wouldn't make it.

Both ways of telling a story are acceptable, but a third person *single* point of view is preferred. Most stories and books are told from the third person point of view because readers are more comfortable with it. So unless you feel your story *must* be told from your personal point of view, it's better to use the less personal third person.

Writing Exercise

Plot A Story

Some students may have a story plot they want to develop. If they have no plot idea in mind, they may choose an "Opening Problem" from the list below. Remind all students to follow the plot diagram and "what if" their way up the diagram until they have plotted their stories.

Remind them not to be concerned if their first story plots are not *great*. That doesn't matter. It only matters that they follow the diagram and do their best.

Opening Problems

(Plots may be developed from any point of view, male or female. A character's names may be changed to suit the writers.)

Ellen learns that someone at school has told a lie about her, and said she cheated on a test. Now, she's in trouble. Who did it? And what will she do?

Sam's mother will be having a birthday soon and he has not saved any of his allowance. He spent it all on himself. What can he do?

Cynthia lives next door to a house that is supposed to be haunted. She wants to check it out but is afraid. What will she do?

Roger has found a secret place in the wall of his room, where he can step through and enter another world. What is it like and what will he do?

When plots have been developed, they should be written out, using the example below. This will serve as an outline.

Example

Title: The Three Little Pigs

- Opening problem: A wolf is trying to break in and eat the little pigs.

- Attempted solution: The pigs lock the door.

- Problem Worsens: The wolf blows the house down.

- Attempted solution: The pigs run away and build a stronger house. It is made of sticks.

- Problem Worsens: The wolf blows down the stick house.

- Attempted solution: The pigs run away and build a brick house.

- Problem solved: The wolf can't blow the house down and when he comes down the chimney, the pigs catch him in a pot of boiling water.

Ask students NOT to write their stories until their plots have been read in class. At that time, if they would like to see other ways their plot might have gone, the class will participate in replotting the story. Present this as an exciting exercise because it is. The students will quickly see how to improve their plots.

Sub-plots

Subplots are used in longer stories and novels. A subplot is a second plot which is taking place throughout the story. It is usually not as important as the main plot but is often just as interesting. The subplot often develops because of the main plot.

Example

The main plot of a story might be about a young girl whose family is moving and she's very upset about the move. She does everything she can to prevent it. A subplot might be about her little brother and how he's trying to prevent it, too.

Subplots are not generally used in short stories. A short story sticks to just one plot and two or three characters. Longer stories, however, can have subplots and several interesting characters.

At this point, it is good to know what a subplot is, and understand how it is used, but you will probably not need to use one unless you want to write a longer story, or novel. When that time comes, you will develop your subplot exactly as you did the main plot - by using the diagram to help you.

Chapter Nine

Editing

When you edit your own work, you must read it as if you are an editor or a teacher. An editor is someone who works for a magazine or book publisher and reads stories and decides which ones are best. Read your whole story at least three times and make the changes that will improve it.

Example

Let's say you wrote this sentence:

The sun was sinking slowly in the west as Little Feather arrive home. She could hardly wait to see her new baby brother. So she jump off her horse and ran inside wigwam.

When you read that paragraph, did you find any mistakes? There are three. "Arrive" should be "arrived" and "jump" should be "jumped." In the last sentence, the word "the" has been left out between the words "inside" and "wigwam."

When you edit your own work, read it carefully and correct all mistakes. Editing also means reading every sentence to see if it is as strong as you can make it.

In the first sentence you might ask yourself, "Do I want to say the sun was sinking" or "the sun hung just over the horizon?" Do I want to say "in the west" when everyone knows the sun sets in the west?

In the second sentence, you might ask yourself, "Do I want to keep it the way it is, or change it to read: *Anxious to see her new baby brother, she jumped off her horse and ran inside the wigwam?*

Every great writer edits every page of writing--several

times!—before sending it to a publisher. As a student, you want to edit every page of your writing before you give it to your teacher.

Example

Sue felt sad whn she looked outside. They sky was gray. The air was damp. It was a terible day for a picnic   It was also to cool for the new shorts she bought to wear for the picnic. Now she would be stuk wearing her old sweter and blue jeans agin.

Study the edited paragraph to learn some basic editing symbols.

You can fit a letter in between other letters - or a word between other words - by using a check mark to indicate where the letter should go.

When you need to add a period, use a small x with a circle around it. ($\otimes$). By using this symbol, you won't overlook the period when you rewrite.

If you need to remove a letter, word, sentence or paragraph, draw a circle around it and use the symbol that means "delete:" (   ).

A line leading from one part of a sentence to another means "go from here to there."

When you combine sentences and completely rewrite them, draw a line through them and write the new sentence above the existing line.

Rewritten, the edited paragraph would read:

Sue felt sad when she saw the gray sky and felt the damp air. It was a terrible day for a picnic. Now, she would be stuck wearing her old sweater and blue jeans again since it was too cool for the new shorts she had bought for the picnic.

Writing Exercise

Edit the following paragraph and rewrite it below. There are five mistakes. Sometimes two sentences need to be combined to make one strong sentence. Also, some of the weak verbs need to be replaced with stronger action verbs.

Sam saw the old man. He was carrying a box. It was tied with string, but he still had a hard time carrying it. The box sort of jumped in his arms as he walk toward the trash dumpster behind the store. He had a hard time holding onto it when he opened the lid to the dumpster. Sam watched him drop the box inside. He let the lid fall shut. After he left, Sam went to see what the old man had throw away. But before he got there, he knew. He could hear the poor cat crying from inside the dumpster.

Rewrite your edited paragraph. Your rewritten paragraph doesn't have to be exactly like everyone else's. Rewrite it to suit yourself.

Transitions

When you stop one scene and start another, it is called a *transition*. A transition means that you are moving the story ahead to a later time, from one character to another, or from one location or scene to another. The best way to handle a *transition* is to simply skip two lines on the paper, instead of one.

Example

When the recess bell rang, everyone jumped up and rushed toward the door. "Slow down," Ms. Margo said. "You have plenty of time to play."

Wanda and Sharon ran ahead anyway. They needed to set up the surprise.

"Did you bring the hats?" Wanda whispered when they settled back into their seats after recess.

Sharon nodded. "Everything is ready."

In this example, the whole recess scene was skipped because it wasn't important to the story. *Any time* a scene is not important to a story, leave it out and use a space *transition* to get your characters to the next important scene.

Writing Exercise

The following *italicized* scenes needs to be edited. A transition would make the scene move more quickly. Draw a line through the sentences that should be removed.

Bill finished his homework on the bus then stared out the window. His dad promised to be home early tonight so they could watch the game together. Sighing, he sat back and watched the cars passing by. It would be at least an hour before he would be home.

He saw an old beat-up pickup truck pass a white car and almost run the people off the road. Then the white car sped up and went after the pickup truck. It chased the truck a long time before the truck turned off the road.

Finally, an hour later, the bus pulled up to his stop.

"Something smells good!" he called to his mother as he opened the door. "And I'm so hungry I could eat a bear! Is dad home yet?"

Hopefully you would have removed the whole paragraph about the pickup truck and white car *and* the following sentence. These sentences have nothing to do with the main story. Simply remove them, leave two or three spaces, and you'll have a smooth transition to the next important scene.

Chapter Ten

Writing Your Story

Once your plot has been worked out so that you know it's exciting, there are several things you will want to consider before you begin writing your story.

Think about each character. Decide what each looks like and decide how each will talk and move. Think about your character's mood and how to make each character different and interesting.

1) Write your story on lined notebook paper.
2) Capitalize the first word of every sentence.
3) Use punctuation at the end of a sentence.
4) Indent dialogue each time the speaker changes.
5) Enclose all dialogue in quotation marks.
6) Use strong action verbs where you can.
7) Use short sentences during actions scenes.
8) Use longer sentences to slow down the action.
9) Write your story neatly so that anyone can read it.
10) Edit your story at least three times.

Writing Exercise

Write a complete story. Plot, edit, and rewrite it, then turn it in to the teacher. Your story should be at least four pages long if you write it out by hand. If you print it out, be sure to double space for easy reading. A printed story should be at least two pages long.

Prior to reading student stories, refer to "The Most Effective Presentation..." and "Guide for Class Critiques," on the following pages.

Keep Writing!

Even if your first stories are not great, don't quit writing. Remember... great writers are not *born* great writers. They are born as ordinary boys and girls who learn to read and write, and then start writing stories. They practice by writing story after story and using their imaginations to think of even better stories. Most of them never had a book like this to help them learn while they were still in grade school. They learned because they kept trying.

If you keep writing stories and following the suggestions given in this book, your chances of becoming a great writer are much better than you think.

Creative Writing Exercises

- Full-page dialogue scenes with two or three characters.
- Full-page action scenes with one to three characters.
- Allow the whole class to participate in plotting a single story which they will each write, bringing their own style and unique detail to the story.
- Have students rewrite scenes from published books, keeping the same number of characters and following the sentence structure but *changing the details* so that the scene is unrecognizable. Read the published scene and the rewritten scene.
- Two page character development pieces, giving physical and emotional details about a single character.
- Develop several new plots and write complete stories.
- Make a list of ten common verbs and have students use a thesaurus to find five or six synonyms. Compose and read aloud sentences with common, nondescript verbs and ask students to volunteer more colorful and exciting verbs to replace those in the sentences.

The Most Effective Presentation of Your Students' Work

Student stories should be read aloud but the work should be kept anonymous. This way, students with less skill will not be so quickly discouraged and friendship and/or prejudice will not influence the comments. This will also compel students to be more careful with their penmanship and spelling, although spelling and/or grammar errors should *never* be pointed out in a creative writing class.

Another reason for not allowing students to read their own work is that they can read "over" their own mistakes and place emphasis where it should be, whether or not the writing actually supports it.

You may want to select one or more particularly skillful readers or read the material aloud yourself. If you select a reader, or readers, inform them that all work is to be kept anonymous. If workbooks are used, books are to be held in such a way that the writer remains unknown. If loose-leaf paper is used, readers should be given folders in which to place the work.

A writer's identity should be made known *only* by the writer, if he or she chooses to identify the writing as his or her work.

Prior to allowing student stories to be read aloud, review the *Guide for Class Critiques* with the whole class.

Guide for Class Critiques

1) **Take notes.** As work is being read, make notes on what you like about the story and ways you can see to make it stronger or more interesting.

2) **Tell what you *liked*, first.** Begin all comments with "What I liked best (or enjoyed most) about this writing is...." Even if everyone else has commented that "the character was interesting," or "the dialogue seemed real and sounded believable" - if that is what you enjoyed most about the piece, say so. This allows the writer to know where his or her strengths lie.

3) **Make specific suggestions.** Never comment that you think something could be stronger or better unless you can offer a way to improve it. Comments such as "I didn't like it," or "I didn't like the character... or plot," are useless unless suggestions for improvement can be made.

4) **Use specific words.** Begin all suggestions for changes with the words, "*The writer might want to....*" These are important words for several reasons:

- Identifying students as "writers" helps them accept the idea that they *are* writers and are communicating effectively as writers.

- The words "might want" implies that the suggestion may be no better than what the writer has written.

- These words free the student of embarrassment and allow him or her to consider the suggestions with an open mind.

5) **No personal attacks.** Do not allow any student to suggest that the writer is "strange, weird," or even "different" for having thought up such a character or plot. Do not allow suggestions that a story is "dumb, stupid, or silly." Insist that all comments be about the writing and ways to improve it.

6) **Never dismiss an entire piece.** Within every piece is a gem of an idea which can be polished. No piece of

writing should be dismissed as "worthless." Always look for an idea within the piece that, with a little imagination, can be more fully developed and made more interesting.

You can teach your students to become effective critics of written material by asking specific questions, such as:

- What is the most interesting part of this character's personality?
- Are all the characters believable? If not, what might be changed to make them believable? If so, what made them seem real?
- Is the plot believable? If not, what might be changed?
- If you were to develop this character, which part of his or her personality might you want to emphasize... and what parts might you have left out?
- Are there parts of this story that might be interfering with the main plot and could have been left out?
- Were there parts of this dialogue that might have been stronger or made to sound more real?
- Can you see ways that might have made this plot more exciting?
- Can you see ways that might have made the ending stronger?
- What was the opening problem?
- Name the attempts to resolve the problem.
- What was the climax of the story?
- Who was the most interesting character and why did you like him (or her) best?

Other Books by Othello Bach

Fiction

Simon Sees

A Mother to Kill for

House of Secrets

Satan's Daughters

Rail Fever

Trapped

Brimstone Brethren

The Sacrifice

The Taking of Joanna

Nonfiction

Cry Into the Wind

How to Write a Great Story

Life After Trauma and Abuse

Body Designing

101 Questions for God

The Father Within

Grow Your Self

How to Write a Great Story   Othello Bach

Secrets of Successful Writers

Children's

Albert and the Monster

Whoever Heard of a Fird

Snigglefuzzle

Does My Room Come Alive at Night

Hector McSnector and the Mail Christmas Order Witch

Jake Snake's Race

Lilly, Willy and the Mail Order Witch

Monica's Hanukkah House

Snyder Spider's Birthday Surprise

The Biggest Sneeze

The Man With Big Ears

Othello Bach

Othello is a multi-genre author of numerous books which range in scope and variety from suspense novels to children's books to non-fiction "How-to" books. Her memoir "Cry into the Wind," chronicles an abusive childhood, including 11 years in an orphanage.

Although a non-reader until the eighth grade, she wrote and sold her first novel to Avon Books when she was 24. It was published three years later.

Othello often composes music and lyrics to accompany her children's stories, and celebrities Joel Grey, Tammy Grimes and Sandy Duncan have recorded her books and songs.

She is a motivational speaker who loves to share "the tools" that helped her overcome an abusive past.

Othello welcomes all reader questions and comments, email her at:

othellobach@comcast.net

www.amazon.com/author/othellobach

www.othellobach.com

www.whoeverheardofafird.com